LIVE. LOVE. LEO.

Words From Modern Times

Poems by Judge Kemp

DEDICATION

This publication is dedicated to those who write, those who create, and to those who want to share their art and passions with the world. These poems are a collection of my thoughts, ideas, and observations of the ever-elusive pursuits of happiness, but mostly they are the conversations with myself about family, life, social (in)justice, political impacts, LGBTQAI2s+ (Queer), racism, and random thoughts.

LIVE. LOVE. LEO.

ISBN: 978-1-66789-804-9

To my mother Johnola,

and my sisters Sonya and Latonya.

Your love has made me who I am.

TABLE OF CONTENTS

INTRODUCTION

Dale Carnegie said it best, "Do the thing you fear to do and keep doing it... That is the quickest and surest way ever yet discovered to conquer fear."

Fear. That little four-letter word that keeps us from moving forward and holds us back from possibility. This is what I used to think about the idea of writing poetry. It truly scared me. I'm not a poet, so I thought. When the topic was first presented to me, us, in Janna Lopez's virtual writing class, **Unearth Your Stories**, two years ago, my reaction was less than enthusiastic and almost comical. My facial expressions at the time of our initial assignment consisted of, from what I've been told, eye rolls and a snarl. I think someone described it as "stank (stink) face", or that look on Lucy's face from I Love Lucy when she had to do something she wasn't expecting, "Eeeew." I had officially mentally checked out.

In general, writing was something I only did when it was required for reporting purposes in school, it was never anything I would do for leisure. The idea that I would be publishing anything, other than a personal blog post, was scary enough. Poetry was even scarier to me because I always had this preconceived idea that it had to look, feel, and even sound a certain way. What I have learned about poetry is that it can really be whatever the writer wants it to be.

Fast-forward to today.

Joy is the word I would now use to describe how I feel about writing and even poetry. I feel a charge from writing. It's hard to believe that less than a year ago, I would be writing and publishing a book of poems. Through experimentation, some repeated encouragement, and allowing myself to be open to the invitation of what poetry could and can be, I have grown to embrace this beautiful form of creative expression. Daily life has become my muse. I am motivated to create by all things that pull on the senses; the good and bad of urban life, and love and hate of humanity.

Live. Love. Leo. is a collection of 55 poems that I've amassed as part of a long journey of self-discovery and self-expression that started during the beginning of the pandemic in the spring of 2020. This book has been a fun experiment of creativity and vulnerability that I never would have imagined. Through these written pieces, I've addressed my family, social (in)justices towards Black people, politics, Queerness, the love I have for my partner, and even dipped into the darkness of uncertain times.

I'm still learning more about the various nuances of this expressive art form and look forward to sharing more of that creativity with you in the future!

COVER ART

The cover tells the story of my writing journey and provides a hint of what readers can expect to discover.

At the center is the earth, a representation of my (our) global presence and the connection I have with the amazing places on the planet. The coronavirus appears at the top because this is when this journey of my literary exploration began. This global pandemic affected us all in ways we could not have imagined and changed our lives for better and for worse. The raised fist, or Black Power, icon honors my Black, African American heritage. From 2019 to now, these past few years have been filled with so much heartache, pain, and suffering bringing to light the abundance of social injustice in our community. A rose petal heart is love. My love for family, my partner, my friends, and for life.

LITTLE JUDGE

(JR.)

XY

12:26 AM Monday
17th day of month 8 in year 64

expelled from place warm

a sanctuary, a chamber of love, of life
into a space, a world cold, uncertainty, a time of joy

sensations new of air, in light, and smell
a detachment of umbilical nourishment, snip

confirmed se**X**
fingerling digits and appendages checked, snip and smack

cries of pain and fear subside

as voice, female and familiar calls out in exhaustion

give him to me, says she

you are my bo**Y**

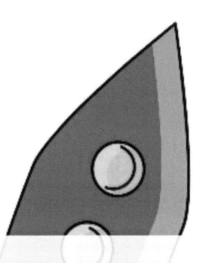

As a Child

As each second lapses by,
thoughts of new adventure and courage weigh on me.

The countdown announces the pending launch.
In 3 ¬-, 2-, 1-...Lift Off!

For what seems like an eternity, the cabin begins to shake.
Then with a thunderous roar, rocket engines push me high into the atmosphere.

As I soar towards the sky the earth grows smaller until it appears
as a distant and shimmering dot floating in a field of black below.

As a child, I dreamt I was an astronaut,
sailing weightlessly through the vast oceans
of space drifting toward distant stars.

Carefully I navigate the constellations,
to safely chart my course through these heavens.

Would I be Lost in Space or seek out new life on my Star Trek?

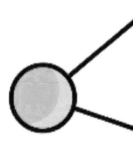

Punching Bag

Dad, you should have been a boxer.

You really know how to work over that punching bag.
With your backhand or uppercut, you were in control.

Did it make you feel like a man?
Bruised knuckles of affection against innocent flesh for your amusement and personal torment.
If you had a bad day, you laid your fists on that beautiful, tanned hide.

When fermented liquids gave you moments of ecstasy and escape, you would hit the punching bag.
Was this supposed to be love?
Was this something grandpa taught you?
Am I supposed to be a boxer too?

From sun up and to sun down the punching bag was always there-safely concealed behind paper thin walls of military housing.

And as another day arrived, it began with words of regret and shaky promises delivered to a nervous heart. But with the night's return, earlier whispers of compassion quickly succumbed to rage as you began to wail on the punching bag.

It wasn't until *MPs came to take you away, was the truth revealed of the violence and shame.

It's been 50 years and though bruises have faded, memories of your actions still stings.

*Military Police

Need help? In the U.S., call 1-800-799-SAFE (7233) for the <u>National Domestic Violence Hotline</u>.

Mother's Love

A breath of life and bond created;

This is a mother's love.

Soft caresses and tears wiped;

This is a mother's love.

A void of hunger and appetite suppressed;

This is a mother's love.

A voice of hope and confidence learned;

This is a mother's love.

Memories shared and experience gained;

For this is a mother's gift.

I Am

I am of a people, culture, and place of far away

I am product of love

I am endless possibility, limited by historical systems of racism

I am of a solo-parent upbringing, flanked by female siblings; one older, one younger

I am of a broader mindset

I am more than myself-global citizen, multi-lingual, educated, and traveled

I am of energy; an empath, susceptible to community mood and emotion

I am self; a proud black man, with a big soul and heart

I am of something beyond stereotype

I am part of the queer community, a gay man who loves without shame or doubt

I am from this place, a City of Roses, a place of 22 years that feels less and less like home

I am of a time before smartphones and internet

I am 50 plus years of then to now

I am of one planet and a human being

WINDOWS & MIRRORS

Ascension

I am awaken from the weighted
　slumber of burden and challenge
　　The guilt, pain, and sorrow of
　　　this life I now leave behind
　　　　It is a new day
　　　　　and I feel light and free
　　　　　　No more concerns
　　　　　　　hold me down
　　　　　　　　And as I rise, I hold hope
　　　　　　　　　in my hands and raise it to my open heart
　　　　　　　　　My spirit soars high with the angels
　　　　　　　　　　love and joy filled the chasm of emptiness,
　　　　　　　　　As I arrive to the golden gates of forever,
　　　　　　　　　　I am turned away
　　　　　　　　　　My time
　　　　　　　　　　　is not yet up
　　　　　　　　　　　　As the invisible force pulls me back down
　　　　　　　　　　　towards the Earth below,
　　　　　　　　　　　　I reflect on my life with gratitude
　　　　　　　　　　　　I am reminded that
　　　　　　　　　　　　　there is more good to do

My Imagination Wants Me to Know

My Imagination Wants Me to Know

That I can travel to any time and place I desire in my dreams; and that

I have an ability to defy gravity with words.

My Imagination Wants Me to Know

My desires allow me to see and experience love; and that

All bad thoughts disappear when I open my eyes.

My Imagination Wants Me to Know

Within my soul, there is my special place of creation and rebirth; and that

It's alright to let my child come out and play.

My Imagination Wants Me to Know

The struggles in my life, are riddles in pursuit of better opportunities tomorrow; and that

Answers reveal themselves once clues are discovered.

My Imagination Wants Me to Know

Feeling alone is just an illusion of self-doubt; and that

A community of friends and loved ones are willing to lift the veil of despair-allowing us to see true beauty in one another.

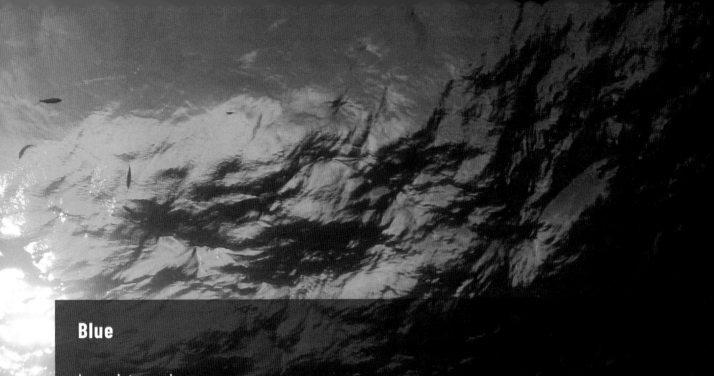

Blue

I gaze into an abyss

Allowing thoughts to float into mind, adrift unanchored to burden

I meditate with breaths calming, my eyes swim in a dark pool of uncertainty searching for answers I already know

Wading into a gulf absent of place forgotten in memory, I ponder liquid shards of rippled fractures casting reflections of open sky

Sensations make me wonder

I seek clarity and peace while navigating whirlpools of dissonance from within and outside my vessel

looking for safe harbor in the distance

I contemplate life and jump into the deep end not knowing whether I will sink to the bottom

Losing sight of light

Losing sight of myself

Never knowing if I'll reach the surface again

Of Love, Of Loss

As life begins

Experience fuels a new mind hungry for wonder and tactile sensation

Senses operate with sponge-like tenacity, listening, watching, and processing the new environment around

Clumsy legs soon find balance in quest of independent discovery

We crawl, we stand, we fall, we run

Words grant us reward

comprehension grants privileges and boundaries tested

Teen time opens hormonal hearts to first crush and first heartache

Maturity defined by number, and wisdom in experience offer both challenge and opportunity

Allowing for chance encounters of a love connection and coupled security

Paired, providing for potential pathways for procreation to parenting

Many happy memories lapse and birthdays past questioning the wondrous life shared

A life absent disease and physical compromise is one of aspiration and yet seldom achieved

The body slows, the mind wanders to an end

This is indeed a wonderful life lived,
of love, and of loss.

Light

Rays of refracted solar dust scattered by celestial forces.

Source of illuminated inspiration, and radiated remedy for seasonal melancholy.

Enhancer of a prism's color spectrum, allowing eyes to see.

A feeling of warmth, touching all within a gaze.

A space opposite darkness.

Cliched expression to dictate mental absence.
(The light is on but nobody's home.)

Symbolic beacon of hope in a time of despair.

Prompter for a rooster's call.

A welcomed sign from a wintery sleep.

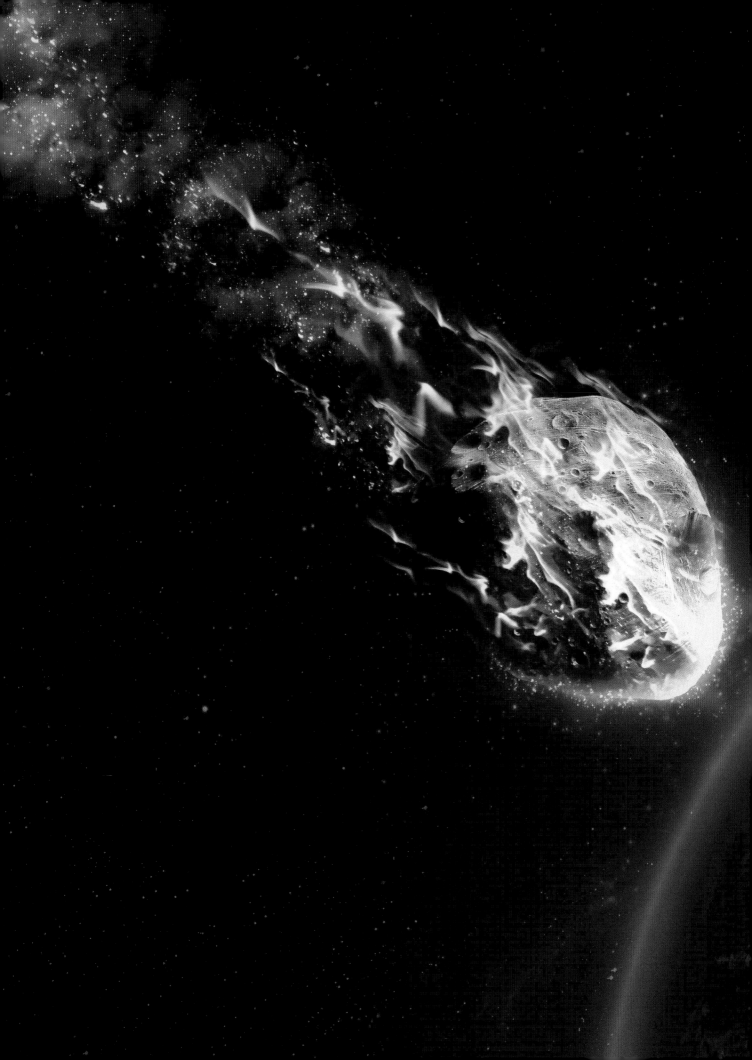

Sky Hammer

Raised is a clenched fist as it climbs
higher and higher into an open sky

With instantaneous speed
the sky hammer falls
Striking places below fast and heavy

Earth gives way to gravity's impression
Creating spaces of organic opportunity
Ground trembles in impact
Exposing forgotten layers of yesterday

Howling winds shriek and dark clouds gather
scattering matter over distances far and wide

Wounded air weeps with salty tears
Pooling vapor into oceans of mysteries deep
Hot rocks quenched in steaming ecstasy
Cooling molten surface into blackened glass

1982, Then & Now

We were in a place of Ebony and Ivory forever resonating in harmony and memory
Looking into the Eye of the Tiger we got Physical

With the progression of Time, I discovered I was a Maneater
whereas other guys were saying That Girl is Mine

In those days, a Vacation was all I ever wanted
Living a life in Freeze Frame as a Centerfold in a new wave magazine
Is this true? Our Lips are Sealed

Then and Now, in a time of 1982
Ronald Reagan was "The Man" who traveled from a west coast to west wing
As our 40th president to be

Struggles old in a new era prevail, as an Equal Rights Amendment
falls short of passage leaving a fight for fairness for another day

In Washington D.C., black granite is laid and etched in tribute to
fallen Vietnam warriors of a far away battle not so long ago

Then and Now, in a time of 1982
In homecoming, we celebrated class royalty with Queen Meridith and King Larry
Applauded "Beatle-themed floats that drifted by on flatbeds clad in shimmery papers, metallic foils,
and iridescent paints: *Penny Lane, Here Comes the Sun, I Wanna Hold Your Hand*

Graduation followed in acknowledgement of academic
achievements punctuated by Grad Night at Disneyland as reward
A night to remember, a time not to forget

We stand here today celebrating a post-Mt. Carmel High School life

40 years of successes, challenges, and personal revelations
Not all could be here in life, in this moment,
but their memories live on through us

Then and Now, in a time of 1982
We are Sun Devils - scarlet red and sunset gold

Redemption

Forgive me I said
There was no malice in the deed in which I've done

Only in truth can we really be free

To live in honor and rest in peace
Absent clutter and guilt

For that is a good life

FREEDOM TO BE

Freedom

I have discovered that the words no longer scare me
The face of indifference no longer frightens me

I am empowered by my own thoughts and dreams
Motivated to find the influences through my senses

Where freedom from doubt opens my heart for adventures to grow
My mind's eye expands to view the possibility of creativity

Allowing fantasy to develop and improvisation to root
Anchoring me to earth and forces wanted to shake my leaves
I have discovered a kinship of likened souls of encouragement

I have discovered that I am a writer

Thinkin About

I'm thinkin about...

The Kaleidoscope of colors in the world and
beauty that exists in life when we really open our eyes

I'm thinkin about...
The diversity and shadows of this global spectrum

I'm thinkin about...
How some colors are hot and others cool or the
safety I sometimes feel in darkness

I'm thinkin about...
Being afraid to step into yellow rays of the sun

I'm thinkin about...
As I close my eyes to hold onto the feeling of hope knowing that
I must face the truth, a truth hidden from myself

I'm thinkin about...
Light as it shines brighter

Exposing my body naked with imperfections

I'm thinkin about...
How I see myself free without shame and without judgment

I'm thinkin about...
The face of compassion I see when I gaze into a mirror to discover my
humanity and love

Tattoo

She was not for sale.

Her body was draped with smooth, velvet-like skin that everyone wanted to possess.

Her lips were full and pouty, tempting to apply your kiss.

Many wanted her and put her statuesque frame high on a pedestal.

For she, like a Queen, was sought after, admired, and worshiped from afar.

Her beauty was a fantasy of their addiction in thought and flesh.

No one will caress this vessel; no one dare feel her without consent.

Her brand, her mark, was now forever present for all the world to see;

I AM WORTHY.

My Ful Life

My mama told me as a child, I was kind and thought-ful, because I would always make funny faces to get her smile when she was feeling down.

As teens, my sisters and I were urged to be respect-ful towards strangers, so we could safely navigate places far beyond our doorstep.

While funds were tight for my single-Ma, I got a job as a newspaper delivery boy waking up at the crack of dawn to be help-ful to my family. There wasn't a lot I could do, but I tried to be use-ful in the smallest of ways.

During high school I heard my older sister, Sonya, sing for the first time and it was beauti-ful. It was a voice that could have easily splintered crystalline glass.

As a young Black male, I was instructed by my mother to be law-ful, citing the high incarceration rates of people who looked like me (us).

Later discovering my own rhythm through dance made me feel art-ful and allowed a chance to gain financial independence and make friends along the way.

Having the opportunity to travel and learn about amazing world cultures made me feel thank-ful for what I have and not what I don't; an opportunity I would encourage everyone to do.

Hearing the words, "you have cancer" made me fear-ful of what that would mean for my health and quality of life. To date, I remain cancer-free.

I am grate-ful for the "Posse" of friends providing fun times, delicious meals, and calm times in chaos. These are the people I'd be stranded on a deserted island with.

I am blessed to have a loving and meaning-ful spouse, partner, and lover on my arm to help steady me when I feel off balance. I am joy-ful of our union that binds us together.

With times seeming so precarious with war, disease, and political discord, I am trying to remain hope-ful for healing and unity. There is no future when we ignore the past.

I have learned that my words can be power-ful tools to tell a story and start conversation. In anger, my words can be wielded as non-physical weapons slicing deeply below skin.

Harm is something never intended. I am always care-ful and thought-ful in how I use my wonder-ful gifts.

Time Traveled

running forward

i backed into you

digits on fingerless hands

tell me where to go and

when to be

a digitized face of expressionless analog

hums in synchronistic unity

i remain a fixed point

gazing into lofty abyss

of a heavy sky

darkness of space is bright

with light of dying stars

at the speed of sound i hear nothing

but my own heart beating

running forward

i backed into you

Vacation

We're embarking on a journey,

To places of wonder and cheer,

Where other languages are spoken,

In locations far from here

We'll travel over lands, across borders, and sea

We'll travel by plane, by train, and by foot, if need be

There'll be beautiful people, of varying shade and hue

People from farther away places, traveling on vacation too

We're embarking on a journey

Where foods won't be bland,

I'll discover new dishes,

Made fresh, with no-thing from a can.

The monuments we'll discover and sites we'll see

Creating special moments for you and for me.

Writing

My electronic pen and paper allow me to speak when my voice is silenced.

Writing is a present I freely give to those I love, allowing me to share my soul;

Writing is a band-aid that patches my heart from social wounds.

Writing opens my mind to fantasy, rhythm, and rhyme.

Writing is expression, an act that transcends beyond place and beyond time.

Writing is the relationship I can't ever quit.

Writing is thought, giving birth to words that live on long past memory.

DISRUPTION

Noise

Dissonance clouds my brain

Making it difficult to focus my thoughts

The cacophony of disharmony within society

Distracts me from what I should be doing

Discord leads me away from what I could be doing

Procrastination further prolongs my task

Pushing duty and obligation farther away

Disruption corrupts silence

Postponing responsibility again for another day

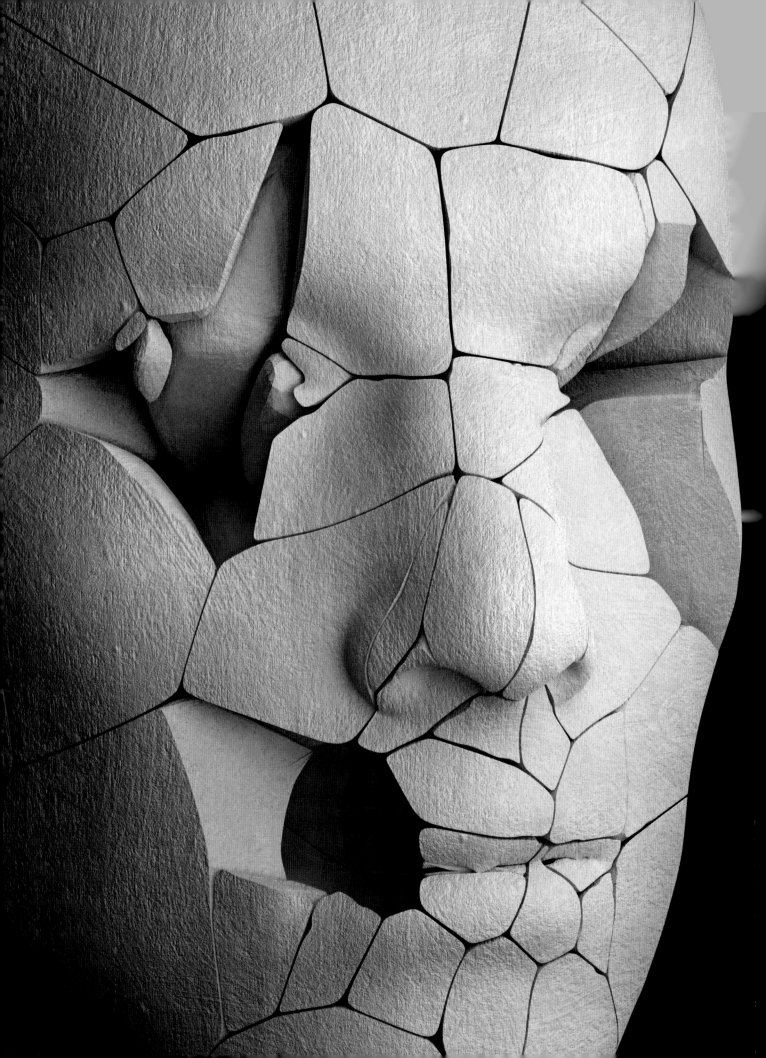

Fractured

Bit by bit

Parts of me chip away

Falling into dust and fade away.

My soul has been battered by the constant attacks breaking down the walls of resistance protecting my heart.

I gaze towards the light, the heavens, in hopes that someone or something will ease my woes; hear my prayers.

I am speechless and saddened by the destruction that surrounds me.

My body and mind are no longer whole.

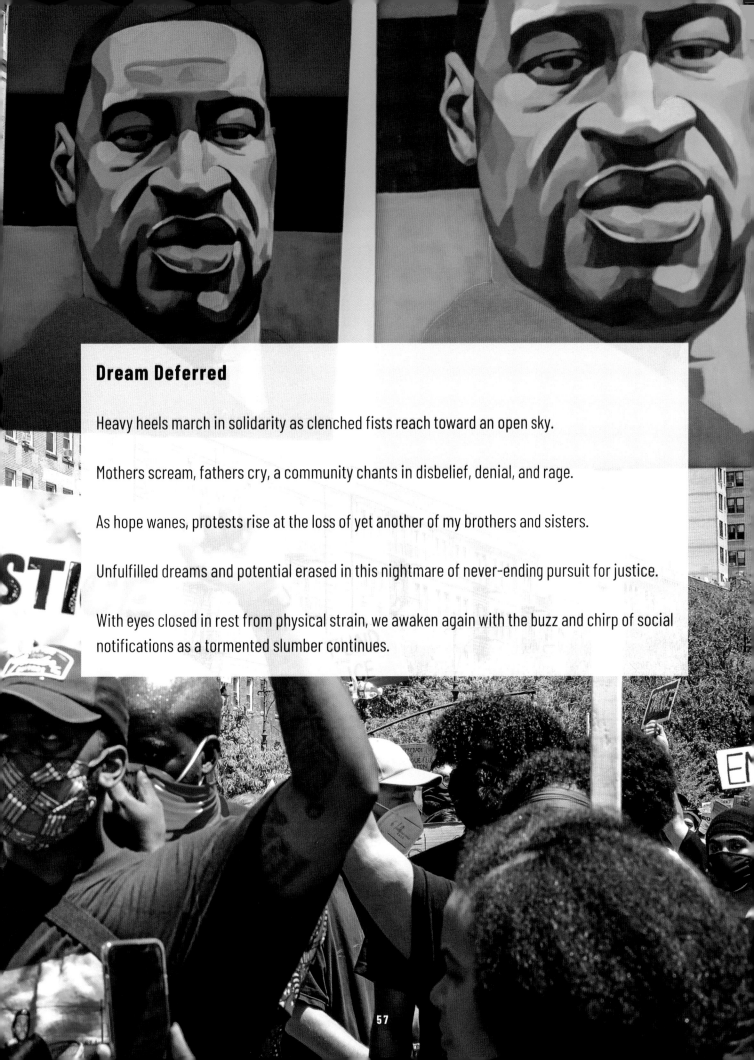

Dream Deferred

Heavy heels march in solidarity as clenched fists reach toward an open sky.

Mothers scream, fathers cry, a community chants in disbelief, denial, and rage.

As hope wanes, protests rise at the loss of yet another of my brothers and sisters.

Unfulfilled dreams and potential erased in this nightmare of never-ending pursuit for justice.

With eyes closed in rest from physical strain, we awaken again with the buzz and chirp of social notifications as a tormented slumber continues.

Red & Blue...

Colors true in a spectral wave of light

Hues used to define and divide who we are

Representing blood and air; the life force of a nation

One left   One right

One good that serves people

One bad that serves self

Topics worn on one's sleeve exposing frayed threads of American civility

Tensions trump common sense, as one group asserts itself over all others

Red and blue

Intentionally placed barriers limit access for some to exercise rights often denied

A hideous abstract painting of the ugliness in this land

Oppressive laws remain death-gripped within fragile white hands,

Reluctantly released after racism's poison has spread throughout the land

Women's health has become less about gender and more about the power of words a man wrote centuries ago to gain religious favors

We the people should honor contributions of all, giving voice to a future of unity and not one that continues to tear us apart.

How Am I?

I'm on edge, again today
Everything around my gaze causes irritation in my mind and spirit
Patience is short with me, so I keep my distance
I stay silent in an effort to prevent me from biting
Prevent me from yelling
Prevent me from wanting to cry
                                        ...again
When will these frustrations end
I'm so tired
and tomorrow's already poised to be a repeat of today

Right now, all I want to do is laugh,
hard enough where the tears roll down my face
disguising the pain and hurt
I want to lose control to the laughter
That uncontrollable feeling when you can't breathe
The kind of laughing that it makes your gut ache
as if you did 1000 abdominal crunches
I want to laugh in amusement and jest
I need to laugh even more than ever
The feeling of relief, that sensation of release,
that desire of satisfaction

Let Me Begin Again

2020 and now 2021.

From a time of confinement and isolation, we struggle to find new ground in today's mystery. Trying to see the dawn when darkness has engulfed much of our light. In one dose or two, it's a remedy of hope to let me begin again.

In desperation and defiance, politics push science into a realm of vulgarity, *Science* has become a dirty word. We try to grasp knowledge in ignorance, where selfishness blinds us and keeps us unwell, unemployed, and unprosperous. Let me begin again.

The warmth of the sun-filled sky pushes away a cold winter dampness. A cycle repeated continuously for a lifetime. The coffee brews in anticipation of the day's connections. Interactions still framed in digital imagery empty of warmth and touch. Sifting through the chats and emojis to feel a hint of hope and energy on the other side of the screen.

Let me begin again.

QUEER & HERE

Glitter*

Speckled refractions

of colors bright

become twinkled amusement

of granular delight

a little sparkle

goes a long way

creates a spectacle of brilliance

that some say is gay

fragments will linger

past a date of use

you'll find tiny shiny remnants

in the crevices of your

caboose

Spoken in your funniest voice.

Election

Dear America(ns):

As one of your 331 million inhabitants, I'm sending energy into the universe where the outcome of the election will bring us all the necessary healing to move forward with our lives and as a nation.

There is much collective good when we come together and unite. For several years, I think we the people have forgotten that this country was the original home of native and indigenous people, a place built by forced enslavement of African people-and a place of opportunity as a Promised—Land.

This is a place of immigrants, LGBTQIA2S+ people, BIPOC communities, and of people representing various religions.

This place, my America(ns), we should never forget who we are or where we came from.

We all deserve the right to be here, be happy, and celebrate life with whom we love.

Sincerely,

Your Neighbor

A Night of Low Standards

In a time before apps...

It had been a while since
I was the object of another's carnal affections.

Feeling the urge
I reluctantly left my confines of walled celibacy and ventured out the door.
I walked to places of flowing libations and inebriated laughter.

New Edition's "A Little Bit of Love" was playing in a bar I passed by.
Was this a sign or premonition of coming events?

I entered a venue and planted myself at the bar.
I conveniently positioned myself where I could see, and more importantly, be seen.
I was in a perfect spot to witness the ebb and flow of "man"- kind as it flowed in and
out the door.

I was out of my element.
I was a fish out of water and I was ...thirsty.

It was Happy Hour and I hadn't yet started smiling.
Two-for-one drink specials caught my attention.
I sucked down a couple of Long Island Iced teas to soften nerves.

My shyness waned as a handsome hottie in a 3-piece made his way towards the bar.
I felt my *courage* swelling.

Our gazes connected.
I dove deep into a deep abyss of his brown eyes.

I was hooked.

Flirtatious conversation ensued and then a hand on my knee.
He wore a wedding ring, but I didn't care.

Tonight the drought is over.
Even I have nights of low standards.

We Are Here

A diverse spectrum of *"family"* bound by blood and not,
representing all color shades in celebration and unity;

365 days a year, 24 hours a day, and 7 days a week;

Forces old, clad in angry habits of righteousness, condemn my life, and whom I choose to love;

Governmentally politicized and medically deprived, we were forced to Act Up.

Voices young and inexperienced in life's journey, demand change now, while ignoring lost souls of a time when.

A place of brick and mortar is now a Stone Wall monument and genesis to the start of a movement.

We are Here

Ridiculed, stereotyped, and victims of violence, our community rallies onward.

From Lesbian, Trans, Dykes on Bikes, Drag Queens, Muscle Daddy Bears, Two-spirit, Gay, and Bi, here is something for everyone.

For this is Pride, a yearly spectacle of parades, sequins, and waving rainbow flags letting the world around us know that... **WE ARE HERE.**

#pride #gay #blacklivesmatter #translivesmatter

THANK YOU
THANK YOU
THANK YOU
THANK YOU
THANK YOU
THANK YOU
THANK YOU
THANK YOU
THANK YOU
THANK YOU
THANK YOU
THANK YOU
THANK YOU
THANK YOU
THANK YOU
YOU
THANK YOU
YOU
YOU
YOU

In Gratitude

In gratitude we honor the original landholders of this country.

Though times have changed and the story altered, we gather.

I acknowledge the labors spent by many so we may savor Earth's bounty.

Bellies will soon be filled and bodies nourished with calories in abundance.

In gratitude, I breathe crisp fall air that fuels my soul and heart.

We are reminded to be thankful for what we have and what (or who) we hold dear.

I'm in Gratitude.

Humbled by smiles and love that have kept me stable when the world is in chaos.

COVID-19 is in the past, but violence against the Queer community prevails.

In gratitude, I sleep sheltered and protected from abuses of the elements.

Grateful to have a home, a space open to family and friends.

A place of safety and tethered facial barriers no longer hide smiles and muffled words.

In gratitude, kindness, hope, and happiness define who I am.

I am compassion. I am empathy. I am a Human Being.

In gratitude I say to all, Live well. Live wise. Live true.

LIVE. LOVE. LEO.

The Big If

And...Action!

If your life were a movie,

What kind of movie would it be?

A science fiction, a romance, or perhaps a documentary?

Would your movie be set in the present day, a future time, or distant past?

Would it be printed on celluloid, 8mm, or on digital format for something that lasts?

Is your movie only a private screening, or open for all to see?

Or perhaps it's a little naughty, like a porno with an X-rating rather than G?

Would your movie take place in a city or sprawling farm?

Where you'd need lots of space to blow things up without doing any harm?

If your life was a movie, who would you cast to play your part?

Do you envision Meryl Streep, Viola Davis, or Kevin Hart?

One final thing that many want to know

Is the title of this epic with a catchy name and flow.

The End

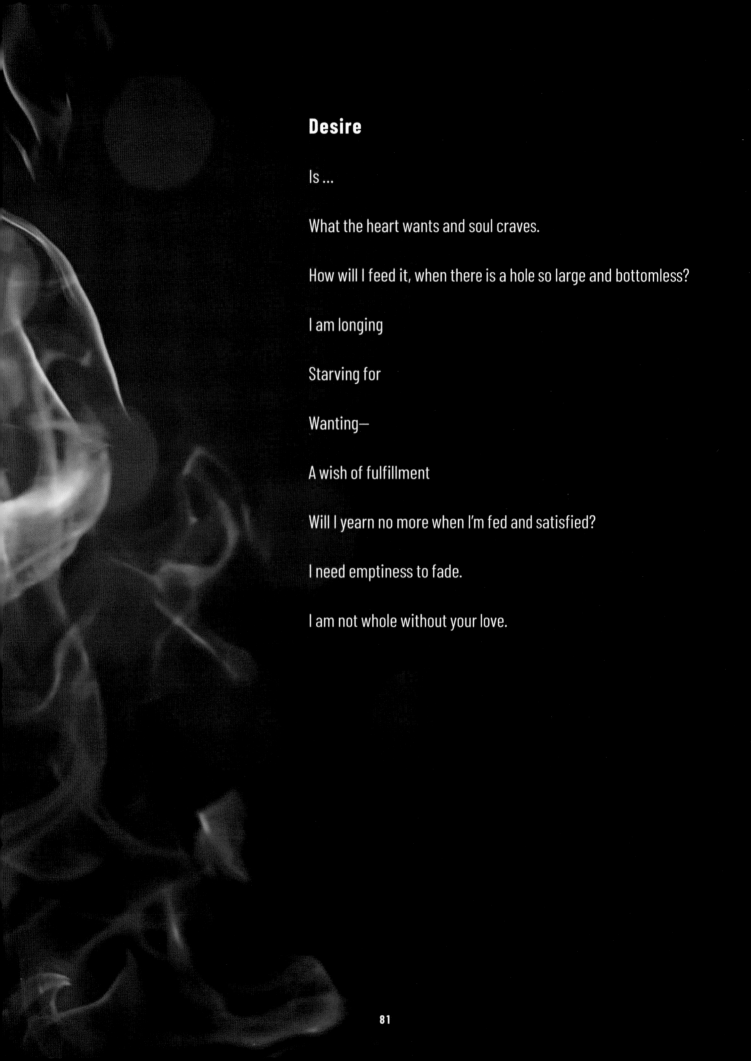

Desire

Is ...

What the heart wants and soul craves.

How will I feed it, when there is a hole so large and bottomless?

I am longing

Starving for

Wanting—

A wish of fulfillment

Will I yearn no more when I'm fed and satisfied?

I need emptiness to fade.

I am not whole without your love.

Birth Pride

Lives written in stars, etched on a celestial chalkboard

Punctuated in the northern sky between Cancer and Virgo

This is a moment, a time of year when we honor, rejoice, and celebrate life

Candles ablaze, glow and dance with schizophrenic choreography
burning in tribute to one's past, present, and future life

In a huff and puff, flames of time are Extinguished
leaving ghostly wishes adrift in air

Wishes of health; wishes of love; and wishes for a better life are embedded in social constructs

Prompting reflection and thoughts of simpler days gone by,
contemplation of deeds and desires in life made worthy

We are a pride of people fiercely loyal, tenaciously helpful,
and Often generous to those we hold dear

What will the next trip around the sun bring?

We are Leo

REMEMBRANCE

Is...

Receiving your first paycheck from a new job and feeling like a grown up

A scented whisper of deja vu triggered by the shadowy specter of yesterday's memory

Your first sip of beer to tease one's palette for future alcohol indulgence

Are...

Once forgotten dance steps awaken a stiffened body into rhythmic motion when hearing a favorite tune - One-Two-Three & One-Two-Three

REMEMBRANCE

Anticipation of true love's first kiss

Is...

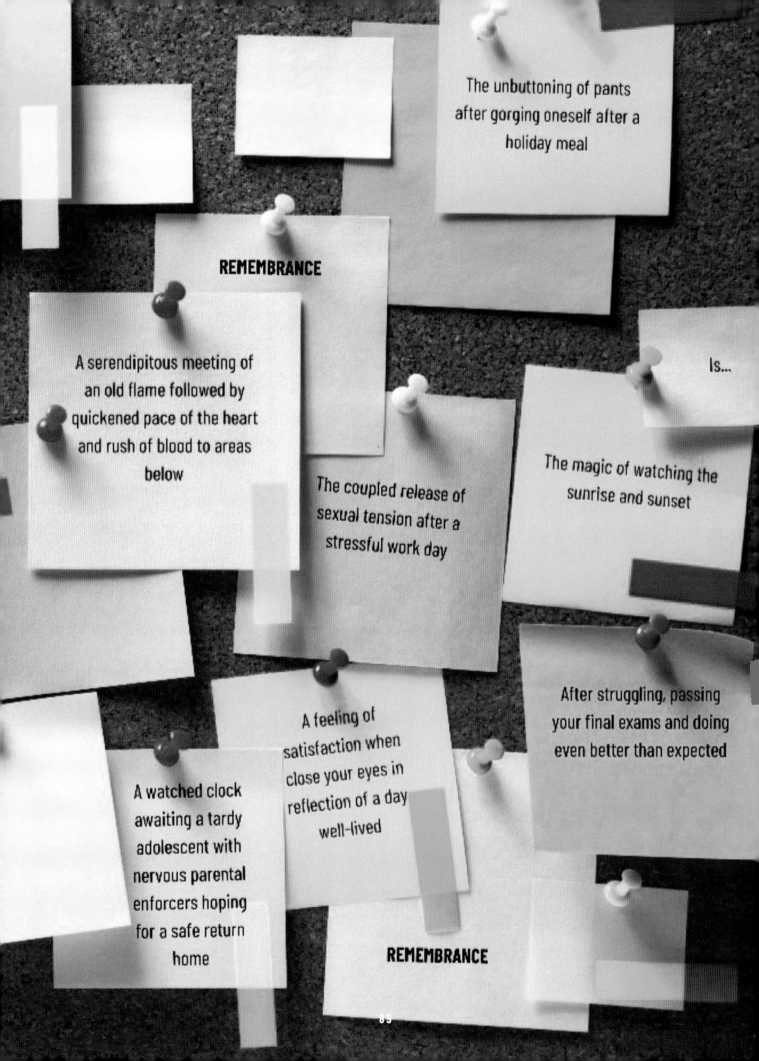

The unbuttoning of pants after gorging oneself after a holiday meal

REMEMBRANCE

A serendipitous meeting of an old flame followed by quickened pace of the heart and rush of blood to areas below

The coupled release of sexual tension after a stressful work day

Is...

The magic of watching the sunrise and sunset

After struggling, passing your final exams and doing even better than expected

A feeling of satisfaction when close your eyes in reflection of a day well-lived

A watched clock awaiting a tardy adolescent with nervous parental enforcers hoping for a safe return home

REMEMBRANCE

Determination

Before me I see a wall, large and wide

It towers over me, casting shadow and consuming light

I'm blinded and lost trying to find points of recognition

Cries for help go unanswered, I feel I am alone

In silence a voice tells me to climb for fear will keep you in darkness

The voice is calming and familiar in tone

I begin my ascent not knowing how high I must climb

Fatigued, I lose my grip and fall back to the space below

You got this, the voice says

In a moment of clarity and focus, I climb

Higher and higher towards the perceived heavens as light begins to shine on me

As I reached the summit I was greeted by the dawn of a new day

It was all a dream but the spark of determination was real

My Holiday

A moment to celebrate me, myself, and I

A time to raise a glass to toast achievements and accolades

A time of unity and embracing my childlike silliness

A time of gathering friends and sharing great food and happy memories

My holiday is...

Non-denominational, non-racist, and non-presidential

I honor the everyday man/woman, not the one who puts him/herself above others

My holiday is...

Not one of sacrifice and honors collective contributions of diverse community

I honor the colors red, white, and blue

I celebrate ancestry in hues of green, red, and black

I party with mirrored balls, red dresses, rainbows, and drag queens

My holiday...

Doesn't "whitewash" historic events of oppression and construe them into rosy-false traditions

But acknowledges faults of fore-fathers as opportunities and forgiveness to grow from

My holiday...

Isn't only anchored to one day a year

H.O.P.E.

H = Is happiness in spirit and body;

O = Is optimism I see in life when things appear dark and in despair;

P = Is pride I feel as I thrive to be a good global citizen;

E = Is empathy that guides my hands and softens my heart, allowing me to feel and love.

IN THE CITY

I Go

I am awakened

from a daydream of night meeting a new day

Somber is my mood, giving way to silence loudly announcing dawn's arrival

I move through the house

Quietly assembling garments of conformity as I go out the door

I greet a friendly feline returning back from points unknown

A life of care-free caterwauling and comfort, I think to myself

In hastened pace I go

With slow legs moving faster I reach my point of transport into the city

My train is shared by others; addictive afflictions scream at the spectred reflections that haunt their gaze

I go on my way to a place of concrete and steel

I go to a place that provides income and employment

I go

I go to work

Rain

F
A
L
L
I
N
G,

downward from points on high.

Landing,

on thirsty grounds heated from summer's rage.

Deluge,

splashing down on dusty pavers

exploding like shards of liquid glass.

Raindrops,

strike the metal roof

like tiny hammers on a piano

creating a hypnotic lullaby.

Branches,

made heavy with precipitation

bend and bounce in gratitude for a gift.

Air,

rinsed clean from the season's smokey end

smells sweet again after nature's shower.

Rain,

trickling slow and silent

leaves behind puddles for juvenile amusement.

much of the country lands have been reclaimed from the North sea
A city of canals and carnal liberation
waking this prudish gay man, from his sexual hibernation
There are coffee shops a-plenty and not a cappuccino to be seen
but you'll get served a menu, with pungent varieties of green

Life in this place, has given great memories and tears,
including performing in Gay Games in an arena full of queers
Your city's quaint and picturesque, and landscapes oh-so-charming,
With buildings that lean, to an architect, that's alarming
This city's truly wondrous, with so much artistic history
Where works of Van Gogh and Rembrandt, are at the Rijksmuseum to see
Amsterdam, my sweet Amsterdam, is a city I long to be
Where tulips, clogs, and, Heinekens, would always welcomed me

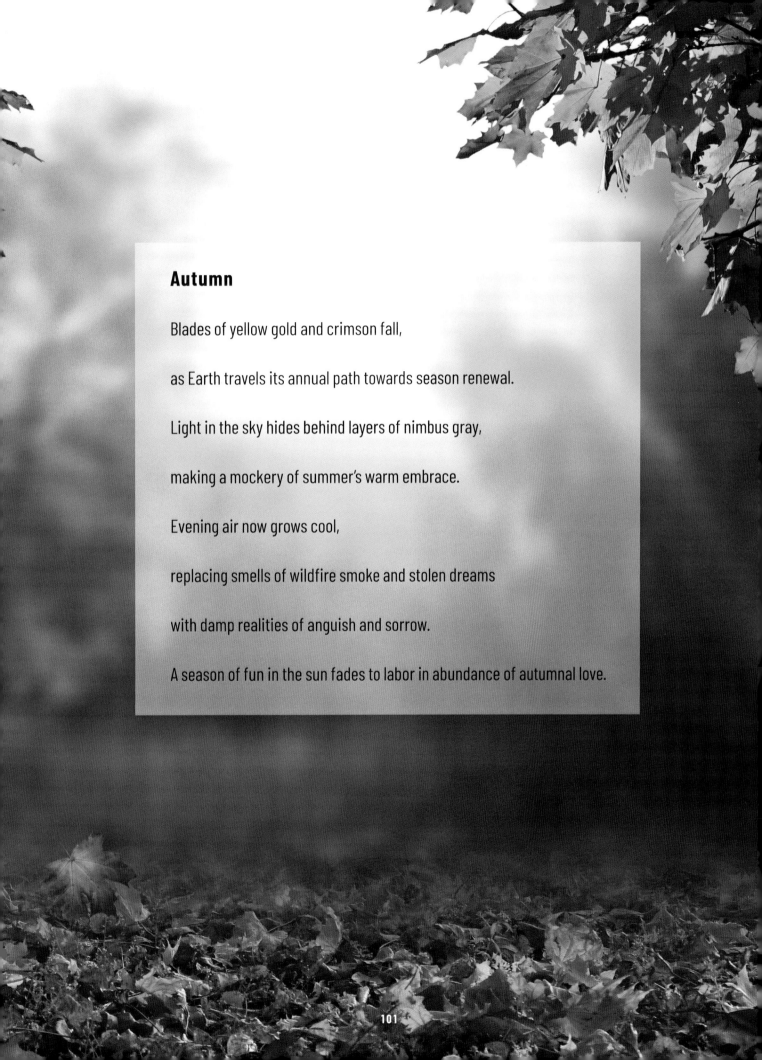

Autumn

Blades of yellow gold and crimson fall,

as Earth travels its annual path towards season renewal.

Light in the sky hides behind layers of nimbus gray,

making a mockery of summer's warm embrace.

Evening air now grows cool,

replacing smells of wildfire smoke and stolen dreams

with damp realities of anguish and sorrow.

A season of fun in the sun fades to labor in abundance of autumnal love.

Commute

Heading southbound into darkness of morning
I cautiously look around
seeing only my reflection in mirror-like windows
In the black-tinted conductor's cabin
is a construction worker, seated a few aisles back
The train is strangely empty and that's okay
Warm summer days make for acrid travel experiences

        Advisory bells chime

the train crosses an intersection warning pedestrians
of the arrival of the mighty MAX (Metropolitan Area Express)

        Advisory bells chime

Stations: Skidmore, Overlook, Alameda are now points behind me
An announcement is heard on speakers; "Be alert report issues of concern"
Luckily, it's not one of "those" mornings
This day, at this hour, the city is peaceful

We arrive at the Sports complex aglow with team pride, though no events are scheduled
After what seemed like a minute, the train pulled away from the station
Making its way over the 100-year-old Steel Bridge, the train lurches and lumbers
In the back of my mind I hear, *I think I can, I think I can* as we arrive to the other side of the river

The next stop is a former Greyhound station where a billboard overhead, advertises a grocery
chain inviting onlookers to shop here; chicken is on sale

The MAX moves again slowly sliding on shiny wet rails like a dew-kissed snake as we make our way
into the heart of downtown Portland
Food carts closed and buildings boarded up welcome us as we pull into Pioneer Place

The next stop, City Hall, is mine,
My day begins

Yuletide

Ashy skin is an indicator of frigid temperatures outside, before I even walk out the door.

From my tinseled-top to my jingle bells, my mocha choca-lotta hide is grayed and itchy.

I moisturize, but there never seems to be enough moisture to quench my thirsty dermis. Lubriderm, Vaseline, and other lotions provide temporary soothing relief.

Mundane TV programming is replaced with old classics of black and white and Hallmark new; encouraging us to remember the true spirit of the season and to be kinder to one another.

Our auditory airwaves and video portals become flooded with rapid-fire holiday ads, to relieve us of earned income for capitalist gains.

Moving beyond the threshold of my home's warm radiant floors and stepping into cold, my nose stings as chilled oxygen fills warm lungs.

Streets usually bustling with activity are quiet and sparkle under a layer of ice crystals glistening in evening twilight.

The smell of fresh cut evergreens, scented peppermint, cloves, and cinnamon dance throughout air like sugar plum fairies.

In the silent night, the modern day carol enters my brain, that makes me want to hurl my eggnog, and fast forward to the new year, "All I want for Christmas...", you know the song, in fact we ALL do.

That's right my friends: it's that most wonderful time of the year again...

Heritage

I am from stolen people and from a place far from here.

I am a descendant of slaves born into a legacy of social unrest and oppression.

My communal body has been beaten.

I am part of a new generation of hope gifted with compassion and empathy.

I am but one man filled with optimism and driven by desire.

I am a dream of forgotten slumber.

I am the first in my family to achieve academic success.

My life today is connected to the past while reaching for the future.

I am a blessing of parental intercourse, the gift, the joy, and the love.

Messenger of Hate

Asshole messenger driving around in support of hate.

I will never understand people like you.

My mind is open to a broader understanding of those who think differently.

I and people like me, only want to live, love, and prosper.

Your sign of hate was small but clearly visible like a baby on board placard intended to catch attention.

I looked in disbelief and then again to confirm what my eyes had gleaned.

"Make Racism Winning Again"

Fuck You Fuck You Fuck You!

My heart sank.

I avoid coming to the westside.

Traveling miles of crowded asphalt and toxic exhaust, as I make my way to meet a friend.

No longer am I in comfort of a liberal bubble.

Thoughts of immediate safety drifted in my mind

but I took comfort in daylight's reveal.

Night would have generated fear and intimidation.

I moved to no longer be in sight of your printed declaration proudly displayed on your rear window.

I stepped on the accelerator; putting you and the poison you represent behind as you disappeared from my rear view mirror.

You are a part of my metaphorical journey.

I move forward and you remain in the past.

Cowards cling to outdated hate while shielded by old amendments that perpetuate denial.

But today is mine, as is tomorrow.

I won't allow small-minded bigots like you to remain in my way or hold me back from my destination.

Less Than

I am a commodity sold and traded
I am not seen as human, not seen as equal
I am devoid of feeling but a source of physical labor

I am forced to have less than and work more to survive
I have no wealth to build a legacy, no 40 acres, no mule
I am shackled with history that's branded on our backs

We are puppets to the majority, used for exploitation
We are called animals, we are told we're no good
We are vilified, falsely accused, and imprisoned
We've been drugged by your powdery poison to suppress us into submission

I wear marks of your justice on my neck; 9 minutes and 29 seconds
I cannot run for leisure, without assumptions of guilt
My resemblance to others doesn't give you the right to detain me
The tool of enforcement is often the instrument of death—intentional or accidental

Saying that our lives matter doesn't mean your lives matter less

Learning about atrocities of racism at the hands of your ancestors,
is critical-thinking for understanding and forgiveness

Our quest for higher knowledge is no threat to your existence,
but a complement to our global wisdom

My pride, my honor, and my color I shall take to the grave

I am NOT less than,
I am the dream of my ancestors
I am GREATER than you can imagine
I AM A BLACK MAN

Change

Like waters of time, tides keep moving

taking me away to a place of pain and opportunity;

This life is hard and unfair, but I push forward with the strength of my ancestors behind me.

Change is gonna come.

Storm winds are unpredictable and spray confusion in my ears,

creating indecision and self-doubt; not knowing whether to listen or cover ears.

Change is gonna come.

I shout to be heard, be counted, be valued, but my voice is silenced by the nature of my skin; I am invisible yet singled out as lazy and a thief when convenient.

Change is gonna come.

A system of justice blinded by wealth and influence, uses weighted scales to leave my brothers and sisters behind.

Change is gonna come.

My hopes and dreams want a better life, even as I am threatened with violence for doing no harm.

They say change is gonna come,

but the question is when?

My Blackness

My Blackness Is...

Often defined by others opposite of me
Misunderstood, stereotyped, and fantasized

My Blackness Is...
Centuries old and born of land far away
Kingdoms rich in hard rocks exploited

My Blackness Is...
Who I am, Gay, Honest, filled with empathy

My Blackness Is...
Vulnerable, with an aching heart witnessing oppression and poverty in streets roamed by those
less fortunate

My Blackness Is...
Not a weakness, but a collective strength of history untold

My Blackness Is...
Not about an amount of melanin that covers my muscular frame

My Blackness Is...
A gift of endless possibility, boundless creativity, and compassion for humanity

My Blackness Is...
Limited only by my own unwritten destiny

HOME IS WHERE MY
HEART IS

Sight

No longer am I in a haven of fantasy or flight and see
the darkness encompassing me.
In this space, there are things familiar, and I see a
man battle his demons for control.
Rabid creatures of the night I see scurry across
roadways in search of sustenance.
In the distance, I hear screams of addiction calling
to yet another victim and then see the aftermath of
orange caps and spent needles beneath my feet. I see
shuttered commerce around me from a pandemic
legacy, becoming palettes for profane expression.
Broken car glass lay scattered on the ground like
diamonds in random display.
Around me I see an abundance of human opportunity
giving in to despair.
In a doorway I see a flickering flame and rancid smoke
rising from silvery foil in the chase of the dragon. I
see sidewalks covered in sheltered fabrics stitching
together a patchwork of forgotten hope.
Once fragrant as a rose, I see a place that wreaks with
the stench of chemical pharmaceuticals.

My tired eyes grow weary and afraid to close. If I let my
sight rest, what will I see when my eyes open again?

Hitchhiker

My destiny is in my hands.

Points north, south, east, and west-open to explore.

The mystery of the road and thrill of adventure call me.

These boots are made for walking, but with flat feet, only for a mile or two.

Some may think me a deadbeat; others as courageous because I live in the here and now, not confined by normalcy of 9 to 5.

The highway won't judge as I travel along endless surfaces of asphalt and concrete.

In the warmth of the day, heat trails hover on the horizon-call me with hypnotic invitation of a mirage to keep moving.

Trust is currency on these hardened byways; a legal tender I wield freely in exchange for comfort, conversation, and memory.

My pockets are full of optimism and hope-feed humanity with positivity knowing I won't end up on the road to despair.

Here I sing loudly and poorly in an open-air theater.

My audience of dry brush and stone will never complain, though a coyote may join the serenade of nature's harmony.

Where will the journey take me?

Places near or far, places familiar and unknown.
My spirit will be my guide and tells me I have arrived when I am home.

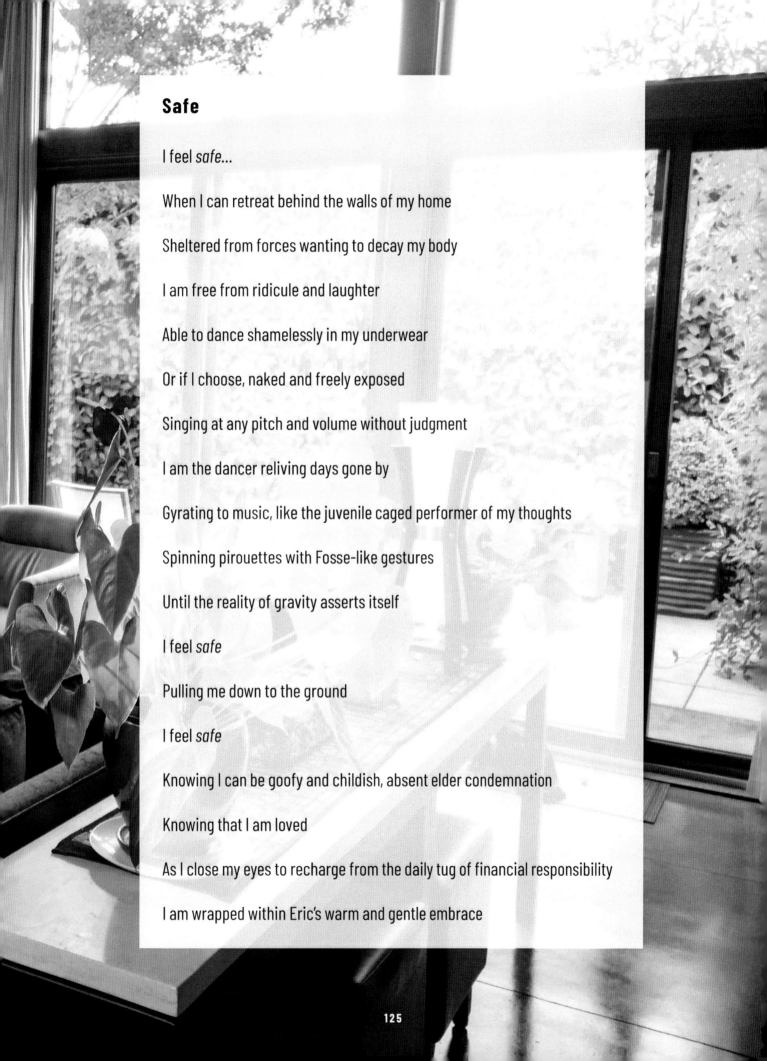

Safe

I feel *safe*...

When I can retreat behind the walls of my home

Sheltered from forces wanting to decay my body

I am free from ridicule and laughter

Able to dance shamelessly in my underwear

Or if I choose, naked and freely exposed

Singing at any pitch and volume without judgment

I am the dancer reliving days gone by

Gyrating to music, like the juvenile caged performer of my thoughts

Spinning pirouettes with Fosse-like gestures

Until the reality of gravity asserts itself

I feel *safe*

Pulling me down to the ground

I feel *safe*

Knowing I can be goofy and childish, absent elder condemnation

Knowing that I am loved

As I close my eyes to recharge from the daily tug of financial responsibility

I am wrapped within Eric's warm and gentle embrace

Lemmon

In counties Stark, Adams, and Perkins, this fruit grows bittersweet;

It's a place juicy in memory and ripened with family heritage;

It calls loved ones home.

Heavenly skies of azure blue, with zested white clouds, dance on an endless horizon;

Roads pitted with dust and rose-colored gravel, chase fields of corn and happy golden flowers;
as it calls loved ones home.

Lands, North and South, split by rail, are enriched with metals of gold and bones of beasts infused
into Native soil;

A homestead with a once mighty river is deep with childhood fun, now flows as a constricted creek
until winter's frozen pour;

Fields of grazing Angus and Herefords bred, provided commerce and recorded legacy;

A marketplace of agricultural retail that once celebrated a hometown world champion;

calls its loved ones home.

Old growth wood now ancient stone, providing a point of entry and curiosity;

A former tavern is given new life and is resurrected into a gallery for artistic creativity;

In Lemmon, South Dakota.

This is a place of unknown history, harmony, and hardship.
A place built of labor and tradition; a place that calls its loved ones home.

Field of Dreaming

In this field of plenty I walk towards the rising sun.

I listen to sounds around me blending into unsyncopated harmony of a new day. I hear sounds of various birds greeting neighbors, and the hum of modern life as cars and farming equipment head for destinations unknown.

I am a stick in the field of plenty; casting my shadow as a sundial forecasting time upon grounds below me. A curious honey bee buzzes around me as a jet airliner flies overhead.

I look around the field of plenty, the colors of grasses and distant trees show signs of seasonal change. Scorched leaves appear ready to fall from summer's extreme heat.

I close my eyes and feel warmth from the sun's rays on my face as coolness of air gently swirls around my body. I feel safe in this moment of mystery and what the day will bring.

I breathe in. Fresh air fills my nostrils with faint hints of my *Aqua de Gio* cologne. The field of plenty is a place of abundance. I imagine centuries ago this was a place of native communities teeming communities teaming with life and activity. We are guests on this land.

Silence is shattered by the honking of migrating geese soaring to graze in a distant field. Crisp morning air awakens my soul and heart. I'm grateful for nature's bounty. Something I rarely make space or time for. So much happens in a moment of observation and reflection. The history of agriculture is etched in the grounds here. A frog croaks in meadows close by.

I change my physical stance eastward to face the sun. When I close my eyes, I see the sun's red-orange refraction through my eyelids. I open my eyes, gaze down at the grasses at my feet, and see more colors than I previously noticed before. The green gives way to yellow, gold, and browns. My body feels awakened by the infusion of a sensorial experience. I hear another plane overhead. When I look up, I notice the plane is an arriving flight to Portland. I'm curious what first time visitors will think of our thorny City of Roses.

I change my position again. Now the field of plenty is at my back. The breeze has increased as the sun climbs into the sky. Cooler weather is welcomed after a warm and long summer. The rustling of leaves from walnut and oak trees sound like a steady flow of water. This place is a haven of hospitality, a sanctuary for one's sanity, and a retreat from the stresses of built environments. As the community awakens, I hear new sounds. I hear the whinny of a horse and occasional sound of a child's voice calling to parents. I wish I had a blanket to spread out on the ground so I could lay back and get lost in the blue sky above.

What a real blessing this place is, in this field of plenty.

With You, I'm Home

I am living in light

Blinded by your warmth

I am dancing in the sun

Bathed in a radiance of you

I breathe in your essence

In your presence I am full

Satiated by your affections

Never hungry for more

Your touch gives me peace

Hands joined brings me calm

A union like circular bonds we wear

Strong like the home we share

Your smile ignites joy within me

Together we shine

Our chemistry is cosmic and erotic

It's serendipitous and comic

Making me glow even brighter with your love

Jealous hearts burn in denial

Singed by hate for who we are
and what we've built together

Open minds grant us safety and friendship

Welcoming us to a place of hope and community

A place to be at home

ACKNOWLEDGEMENTS

Gratitude is a word that describes the many influences around me when it comes to writing. When it comes to this book, I want to thank Janna Lopez for her open invitation to participate and contribute to her Unearth Your Stories writing class (virtual). She really opened my eyes, ears, and heart to writing and its wonderful complexities in creativity. Through her guidance and conversations, she has introduced me to many amazingly talented fellow writers I can now call friends. This gratitude is shared with my fellow course mates for their support and camaraderie.

To my partner and spouse (Eric), thank you for your patience. You have lovingly endured many, many, silent evenings, and weekends of me typing away in the background when we would be normally viewing a favorite television program or other coupled activity. I have always valued your thoughts regarding my writing. I knew I had written something special when, after reading, you asked if I had actually written it. That may sound a tad trite, but I never took your comments as doubt of my abilities, but rather one of flattery for someone experimenting with a new and unfamiliar creative endeavor for the first time. I love that after so many years together, I can still surprise you.

A special thank you to local Portland, OR artist Chris McMurray for lending his talents and creative imagery for the Black Is My Beautiful section. Your artistry and use of color, shapes, and Afro-centric influences made the perfect partnership with my written words.

Follow Chris at:

www.ChrisMcMurry.com
Instagram: chrismcmurrydotcom
Facebook: chris mcmurry the artist

Lastly, I want to acknowledge the readers of my blog who follow my work. Your encouragement and support have continued to fuel my desire to write, explore, and play with words. Thank you for being a part of my personal journey with the written word. I don't have offspring to leave behind as my living legacy to the world. What I do have are my thoughts, ideas, and written words. Words that I am proudly and unapologetically happy to share and that will remain in conversation long after my name is but a whisper in time.

#communitymotivatedandgloballydriven　　　　**judgedontjudge.blog**